Wealth Of Nations

Nigeria

Jane Ayliffe

WAYLAND

Wealth of Nations series includes:

Bangladesh

Egypt

Ghana

Nigeria

Nigeria is a simplified version of the title *Nigeria* in Wayland's Economically Developing Countries series.

Cover: Foreground: villagers on their way to a festival; Inset: the front of a temple.
Title page: Buying fish from the boats on the banks of the River Niger.
Contents page: The Argungu fishing festival in north-west Nigeria.

Series editor: Paul Mason

First published in 1998 by
Wayland (Publishers) Ltd
61 Western Road, Hove
East Sussex, BN3 1JD, England

Find Wayland on the Internet at www.wayland.co.uk

British Library Cataloguing in Publication Data
Ayliffe, Jane
     Nigeria. - (The wealth of nations)
     1. Nigeria - Economic conditions - 1970 - Juvenile literature
     2. Nigeria - Social conditions - 1960 - juvenile literature
     I. Title
     966.9'053

ISBN 0 7502 2255 7

Typeset by Paul Mason.
Printed and bound by Lego, Italy.

Acknowledgements
Camera Press 42; J. Allan Cash Photo Library 33; Robert Estall Photos 15 (top); Mary Evans Picture Library 12 (bottom); Eye Ubiquitous 17, 22, 35; Impact PhotosCover, 3, 4 (main), 14, 26, 27, 28, 29, 37 (top & bottom); Robert Harding Picture Library 5, 8, 18, 19, 24, 25, 32, 43, 44; James H. Morris Title page, 4 (inset), 34; Panos Pictures 6, 7 (top & bottom), 9, 10, 15 (bottom), 16, 20, 21, 23, 25, 38, 39, 40, 41, 45 (top & bottom); Popperfoto 13, 30, 31 (top & bottom); Werner Forman Archive 11, 12 (top).

CONTENTS

INTRODUCTION

Nigeria is a large country in West Africa. It is so big it is known as the 'giant of Africa', because it has more people than any other African country. It was named after the River Niger, which flows through its centre.

▼ A man from the Hausa tribe.

People have lived in Nigeria for thousands of years. But the Nigeria we know today was only formed in 1960. Over 250 different tribes of people live there, each with their own language, religion and traditions.

Nigeria is one of the biggest producers of oil in the world. This has made many people rich, but most people are poor. They live in the countryside, growing just enough food to eat themselves.

NIGERIA'S FLAG

Green is for the rich land; white is for peace.

▲ A family in a village in central Nigeria.

Nigeria has many natural resources which could make it very rich. But the number of people is growing too fast. This means that there is not enough food, jobs, schooling or health care for everyone.

NIGERIA FACTS

Population: 101 million

Capital city: Abuja

Area: 923,768 km square

Main religions: Islam (in the north) and Christianity (in the south).

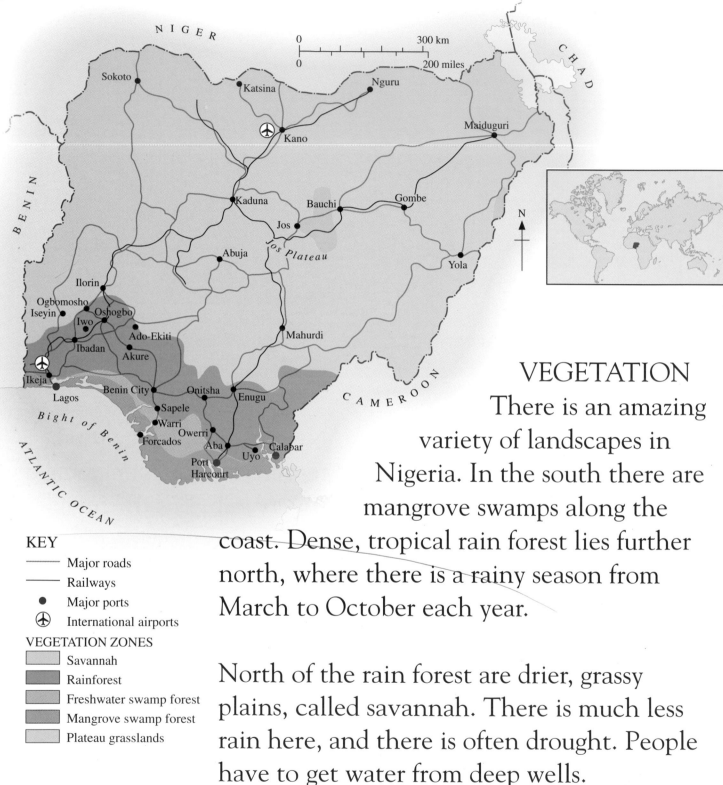

NIGER

Sokoto

Katsina

Nguru

CHAD

0   300 km

0   200 miles

Kano

Maiduguri

BENIN

Kaduna

Bauchi

Gombe

Jos

Jos Plateau

Abuja

Yola

N

Ilorin

Ogbomosho
Iseyin
Iwo
Oshogbo

Ado-Ekiti

Mahurdi

Ibadan
Akure

Ikeja

Benin City

Onitsha

Enugu

CAMEROON

Lagos

Sapele
Warri
Forcados

Owerri

Aba

Uyo

Calabar

Bight of Benin

Port
Harcourt

ATLANTIC OCEAN

KEY
— Major roads
— Railways
●   Major ports
✈   International airports

VEGETATION ZONES
- Savannah
- Rainforest
- Freshwater swamp forest
- Mangrove swamp forest
- Plateau grasslands

VEGETATION
There is an amazing variety of landscapes in Nigeria. In the south there are mangrove swamps along the coast. Dense, tropical rain forest lies further north, where there is a rainy season from March to October each year.

North of the rain forest are drier, grassy plains, called savannah. There is much less rain here, and there is often drought. People have to get water from deep wells.

▶ People getting water from a deep hole in the ground.

In the far north is a dry, dusty region next to the Sahara Desert. People wear long, loose robes to keep them cool.

MANGROVE TREES

Mangrove trees grow on swampy, saltwater coasts all round the world. They have long roots, which anchor the trees in the mud when the tide flows in and out. Nigeria's coast has large areas of mangrove. These are good places for fishing.

◀ The long roots of a mangrove tree.

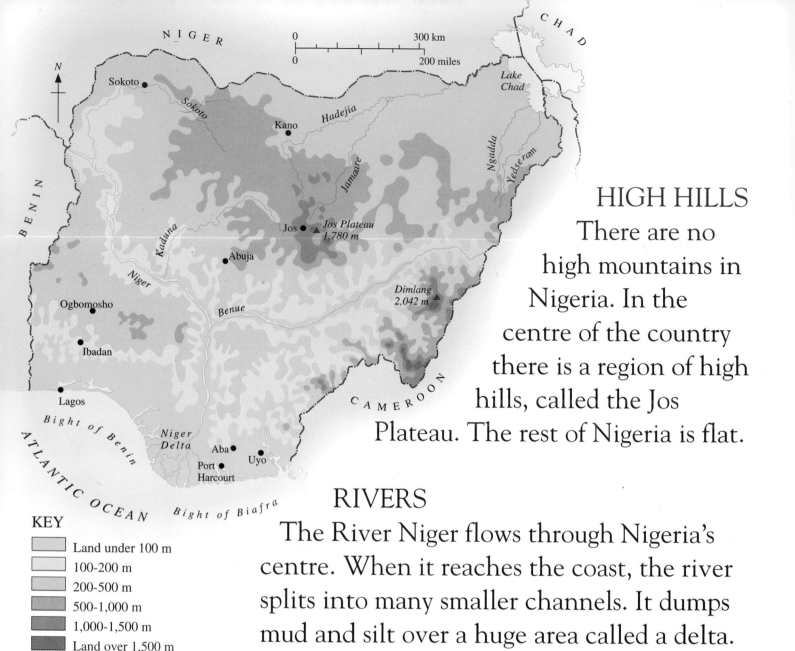

HIGH HILLS

There are no high mountains in Nigeria. In the centre of the country there is a region of high hills, called the Jos Plateau. The rest of Nigeria is flat.

RIVERS

The River Niger flows through Nigeria's centre. When it reaches the coast, the river splits into many smaller channels. It dumps mud and silt over a huge area called a delta.

KEY

Land under 100 m
100-200 m
200-500 m
500-1,000 m
1,000-1,500 m
Land over 1,500 m

▶ Shepherds in the hills of central Nigeria.

► Fishing on the River Niger at Onitsha. Thousands of families rely on the river for their livelihood.

'I catch fish from the River Niger. I sell some in the local market, and the rest in Lagos.' - A fisherman in the Niger Delta.

THE BLACK FLOOD

Every year, the water level in the River Niger rises because of heavy rain near its source. Soon after, the river floods over the flat plains around it.

The water dumps rich soil on the plains, which helps crops grow. But too much water can cause damage to people, animals and crops.

WILDLIFE

Nigeria has an amazing variety of wildlife. Antelopes and gazelles live on the grassy plains, looking out for the lions and leopards that hunt them. Beside them, elephants and buffalo graze. Hippopotamuses and crocodiles lurk in the rivers. In the rain forests there are monkeys, chimpanzees and giant pigs.

Many animals are in danger of becoming extinct as Nigeria's rain forests are destroyed and people take over the grasslands. Some animals can now only be found in protected wildlife reserves.

▶ Elephants in a wildlife reserve.

THE PEOPLES OF NIGERIA

People have lived in Nigeria for over 2,200 years. Yoruba people have lived in the south and west since 900 AD. Today, their ancestors are famous for their weaving, carving and sculpting skills.

Benin and Hausa people had great empires in the east and north. The Benin made beautiful bronze carvings.

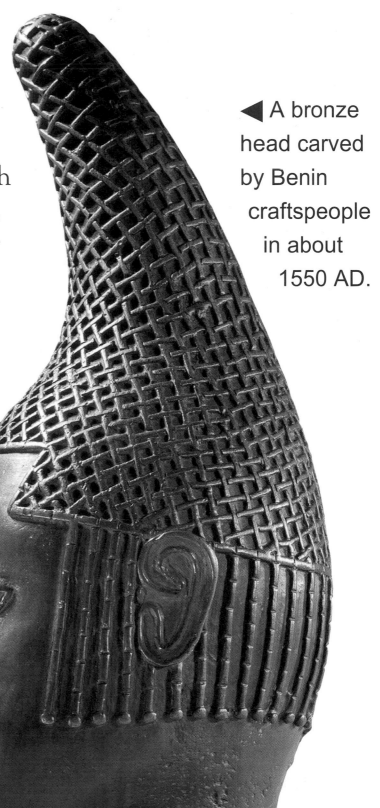

◀ A bronze head carved by Benin craftspeople in about 1550 AD.

11

▲ A nineteenth-century carving.

Portuguese, British and other European countries arrived in West Africa after 1472, trading in gold, spices, ivory and slaves. In 1883, Nigeria became a British colony, until it became an independent country in 1960.

THE SLAVE TRADE

From the 1500s, European countries needed workers for their sugar and tobacco plantations in the Caribbean and South America. They shipped out slaves from Nigeria.

Slaves were prisoners from wars in Nigeria, or they were captured by gangs of slave hunters. Many died on the boat journey to America.

▶Slave hunters taking their prisoners to a ship. The diagram shows how the slaves were packed in.

Once they reached the Americas, the slaves were sold, mostly to farm owners. They were made to work hard in hot, dangerous conditions. Any who tried to escape were severely punished.

SINCE 1960

Since 1960 there have been many difficulties in Nigeria and wars between the people. Most of the time the people have not been able to choose who runs their country. Instead their leaders have been powerful army generals.

CIVIL WAR

In 1967, the Ibo people wanted to rule their own part of Nigeria. So they broke away and named an area in the south-east the Republic of Biafra.

War broke out between Biafra and the rest of Nigeria. Soon, many countries became involved. Millions of Ibo people died during the war.

After three years, the Nigerian army forced the Republic of Biafra to become part of Nigeria again.

▲ Ibo people during the civil war.

▲ A Fulani girl.

NIGERIA TODAY

Over a billion people live in Nigeria today, and they come from many different tribes.

The main tribes in the north are the Hausa and the Fulani. The Ibo are in the south-east, and the Yoruba in the south-west.

The tribes are given money by the government to rule their land. Each state in Nigeria is controlled by a certain tribe.

RIVALRY BETWEEN THE TRIBES

Nigeria's borders were decided by the British in the nineteenth century. Some tribes, who had always been enemies, found themselves living beside each other. Now, they fight each other for power in Nigeria instead of working together.

One way in which the tribes 'fight' each other is by claiming to have a lot of people. This is because more people equals more money from the government.

This has led some leaders to claim more people than they actually have. Because of this, in 1991 the government had to reduce its population figure from 120 million to 88.5 million!

FESTIVALS IN NIGERIA

There are so many religions in Nigeria that sometimes it seems as if every day is a festival for someone!

Nigeria's Muslims dress in their brightest clothes for special sallah-day celebrations, and Christians celebrate Christmas with great feasts.

A favourite festival is held by the Woodaabe people. The men wear face paint and bright clothes. They are all trying to win the title of Most Beautiful Man. At the end of the festival, the women pick the winner!

▶ Woodaabe men in the festival for the Most Beautiful Man.

◀ Muslims going to a *sallah*.

RELIGION

The main tribes in Nigeria have different religions. In the north, the Hausa and Fulani tribes are Muslim. In the south, the Yoruba are Protestant and the Ibo are Catholic.

Some people still practise animism, which is an ancient African religion. Animists believe that natural objects, such as rocks and trees, have spirits.

LANGUAGE

English is the official language in Nigeria, but there are over 400 other languages that are spoken. The different tribes tell their children stories and legends in their own language, so that it does not disappear.

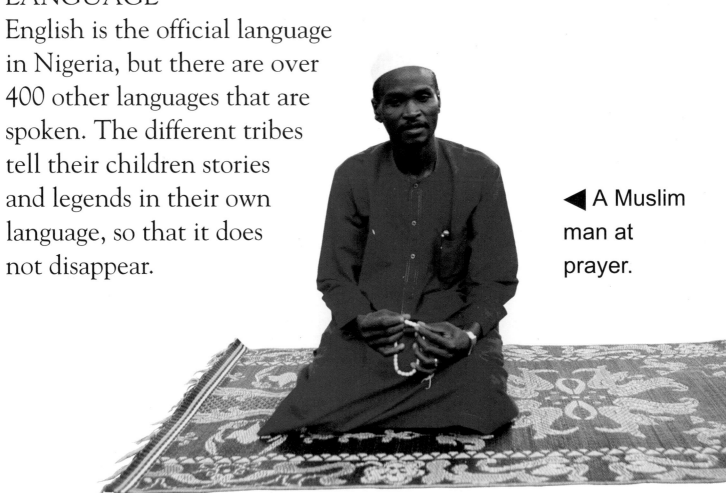

◀ A Muslim man at prayer.

THE FULANI PEOPLE

'The rainy season is very hard. We have to keep the cattle moving over flooded ground. The flies get everywhere,' says a Fulani herdsboy. Fulani people live in northern Nigeria, where they are famous as herders of cattle, sheep and goats.

◀ A Fulani boy herding cattle.

Many Fulani still live in this way, moving from place to place to find new grazing for their animals. They know the land better than anyone else so they always know where to find water. The richest person is the herder with the most cattle.

Other Fulani have settled down to live in cities in the north, where many have become governors, called *emirs*. More and more Fulani are choosing to settle in the cities. Life there is far more comfortable in lots of ways than being a herder.

IN THE CITY

THE CITIES

Most people in Nigeria live in the countryside. But Nigerian cities are the fastest-growing in the world because the population is growing so quickly.

The biggest city is Lagos, which used to be the capital. Lagos is a major port, which grew in the nineteenth century when millions of slaves were shipped from it on their way to America.

▲ Buses on a crowded street in Lagos.

Today, about 1.4 million people live in Lagos, but the population is growing too fast for the city. Poor areas of housing are spreading all around the city. These are called 'popular settlements'.

POOR HOUSING

Many poor houses in Lagos do not have electricity or running water. The drains are open and the rubbish dumps are not cleared, which means people can easily catch diseases.

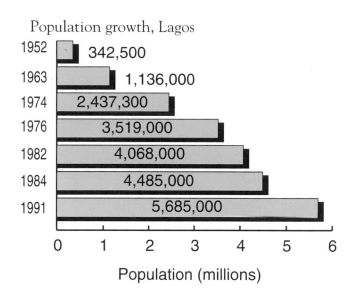

Population growth, Lagos

Year	Population
1952	342,500
1963	1,136,000
1974	2,437,300
1976	3,519,000
1982	4,068,000
1984	4,485,000
1991	5,685,000

Population (millions)

'It can be hard living here. My father is a taxi driver and my mother works as a maid. But there is never enough money for our food, rent, clothes or petrol for the taxi,' **says Chidi Adibeyo, 13 years old, from a slum in Lagos.**

◀ Houses in a poor area in Lagos.

19

TRAFFIC JAMS

All Nigeria's cities are very busy. They are famous for their traffic jams, which are called 'go-slows'. Long lines of cars and trucks often block the roads over whole areas of cities. Drivers can get very angry sitting in their cars.

But some people like the 'go slows'. Street hawkers depend on them for making a living. They walk along the lines of traffic, selling newspapers, cheap televisions and anything else they can to drivers stuck in their cars.

▶The national mosque in Abuja.

◀ These men are trying to sell cheap goods to passing motorists.

20

◀ Houses made of dried mud in the centre of Kano.

KANO

Kano is an ancient city in northern Nigeria, where houses were built from mud bricks to keep people cool in the day and warm at night.

CRIME IN NIGERIA

As parts of Nigeria have been getting poorer, more and more people have turned to crime to earn money.

In Lagos, crime is getting much worse. Robbers and gangs of youths steal from houses, shops and street traders.

Car thieves come to Lagos from Benin, and escape home in stolen cars. Sometimes there are gunfights as the police try to stop the thieves getting away.

There is also a growing drug trade in Nigeria. Drugs from Thailand and Brazil are brought to Nigeria. From there they are carried to Europe or the USA. There they are sold for a high price.

IN THE COUNTRYSIDE

THE COUNTRYSIDE
Most people in Nigeria live and work in the countryside.

The richest farms are plantations, which use modern machinery and fertilizers on the crops.

Only the wealthiest farmers can afford machinery and fertilizers.

Plantations produce crops for sale, not for people to eat. Crops like cocoa, groundnuts and palm oil are sold abroad. Most of the money goes to the government, not to the people.

FARM WORK

People in agriculture	1970	1980	1990
	71%	68%	65%

▲ A tractor on a plantation.

**AGRICULTURAL
PRODUCTION**
(thousand tonnes)

Cassava

Millet

Maize

Plantains

Groundnuts

Cocoa, rubber and cotton

Source: FAO Production
Yearbook, 1992.

20,000

3,200

1,700

1,350

1,214

303

SUBSISTENCE FARMING

Most people in the countryside work on tiny farms, growing just enough food to eat and a little to sell. This is called subsistence farming. They pick the crops by hand, without the help of expensive machinery.

Life can be hard for subsistence farmers. They cannot afford to have a bad harvest.

▼ Women picking a wheat crop by hand.

THE MARKETPLACE

Nigerian markets are colourful places. Lots of different types of food and crafts are on display. People bring whatever crops they have spare to sell.

▼ Bright-red chilli peppers for sale in an open-air market.

Most Nigerians prefer shopping in their local market, rather than the modern shops in the cities. The market is a good place to catch up on the news.

'I love the market. It's a chance to catch up with my friends,' **says Elizabeth Aransi, a farmer's wife.**

In the past, children in the countryside helped their parents work on the land, and looked after them when they grew old. But in the last ten years, more and more young people have been moving to the cities. This means that many older people in the countryside are now left struggling to survive on their own.

▼ Bundling wheat in a northern village.

25

VILLAGE LIFE

The day starts early in the villages. The men work on fields further away, while the women look after vegetable plots closer to home. Women also work at home, preparing food, cooking, cleaning and looking after their children and grandparents. Old people are looked after by their family, so grandparents, parents and children often share a home.

▶ Women pounding yams into flour. Yams are a type of vegetable, a bit like potatoes. They can be cooked and eaten in many different ways.

CHILDREN AT WORK

When the children come home from school, they help by doing jobs such as fetching water.

Many farmers have large families so their children can help them with their daily work.

▲ These children are helping out.

▲ Boys setting out clay bricks to dry in the sun.

VILLAGE HOUSES

Many houses in the countryside are still built using mud bricks. The bricks are dug from a clay pit and left in the sun to dry.

Once the brick are dry, the men start to build the walls. This can be a long, hot job. In the past, roofs were made of reeds gathered at the river. Now, though, corrugated iron is more popular as it is easier to use and more waterproof.

Village houses are laid out in groups called family compounds. Each family has its own compound, made up of a toilet, a shrine, a grain store, and houses for parents, grandparents, aunts and uncles.

CASE STUDY: THE VILLAGE OF EYE-AKAN

▲ These women are making wood fires to dry the pots they have made.

Aye-Ekan is a village of the Yoruba people in south-west Nigeria. Like most Nigerian villages, the main job is farming.

The main crops are yam, maize and cassava, and vegetables such as okra, peppers, tomatoes and beans.

Farming is back-breaking work because there are no tractors or machinery to help. Instead, all the work is done using hand tools.

The main jobs on the land are harvesting and weeding. Children do most of the weeding because is it easier for them to pull the weeds out of the ground.

The women collect water and firewood, as well as cooking and looking after the children. Collecting water is very hard work because the nearest river is 2 kilometres away.

Women also make pots using river clay. The pots are soaked in locust-bean juice to make them waterproof. They can then be used to collect water or for cooking.

The men work mainly at farming. They clear areas ready for planting and prepare the soil for new crops. Different crops can then be harvested at different times.

▶ This woman is shaping wet clay into a pot.

WHY IS NIGERIA POOR?

Nigeria is still one of the poorest countries in the world, even though it has made a lot of money from oil since 1956. There are many reasons for this.

OTHER COUNTRIES

In the past, other countries such as Britain have used Nigeria's food and raw materials for their own good.

When the British found out that tin was being mined in central Nigeria, British companies took over the mines. The money they made went straight back to Britain.

▼ A British tractor at a Nigerian tin mine.

MEASURE OF POVERTY

The poverty of a country is measured by looking at figures such how many people can read and write.

Only 50.7 per cent of Nigerians can read and write. In Britain and the USA, the figure is 99 per cent.

FOOD PRODUCTION

Britain also used Nigeria to produce food which was sent back home or sold abroad. This meant there was not enough land to grow food for local people to eat. In the 1940s, many Nigerians were starving.

▼ A British rubber factory in the 1920s.

The British grew crops such as rubber, cocoa and groundnuts on large plantations. They used machinery to produce large quantities of crops, so they would make more money when they were sold abroad.

▶ A machine taking the shells off groundnuts in a British factory.

DEPENDENCE ON OIL

Nigeria's dependence on oil is another reason why it is poor. Nigeria has relied on the sale of oil since it was discovered in 1956.

When the price of oil was high in the 1970s, Nigeria made a lot of money. Big, expensive building projects were started, including a new capital city, seven new universities and several dams.

When the price of oil dropped in the 1980s, Nigeria had to borrow large amounts of money from other countries to finish the building projects. Now Nigeria is struggling to pay back its debts.

▲ An oil worker with a drill. The changing price of oil affects Nigeria's wealth.

▶ The building of this dam was started in 1968. It cost over $ 250 million.

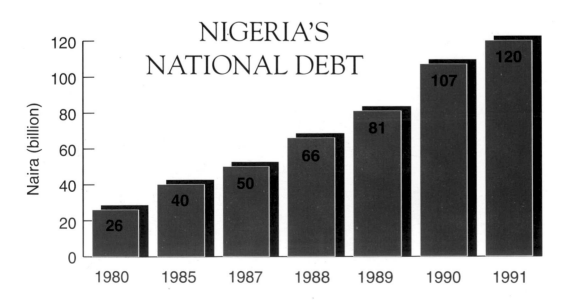

NIGERIA'S NATIONAL DEBT

Naira (billion)

- 1980: 26
- 1985: 40
- 1987: 50
- 1988: 66
- 1989: 81
- 1990: 107
- 1991: 120

FOOD PRODUCTION

Nigeria's dependence on oil has affected its food production.

Nigeria used to be the world's largest producer of palm kernels and palm oil, and a major producer of tropical vegetables and food. Since oil was discovered, most of the government's money has gone into the oil industry, so food production has dropped.

◀ Bunches of palm fruits are collected, to be taken to the oil palm factory.

POPULATION GROWTH

Another reason why Nigeria is poor is that its population is growing too fast.

Nigerians have large families so that their children can help work on the land and look after them when they are old. But as the population grows, there is not enough land or food to feed everyone.

▲ Children in a river village. Most families have six or seven children in Nigeria.

DEVELOPMENT IN NIGERIA

FIGHTING POVERTY

Since 1960, Nigerian governments have tried to improve people's standard of living in different ways. Sometimes they have been successful, while at other times they have not.

DAMS AND IRRIGATION

The government has tried to help farmers grow more food by building dams and irrigation systems. Irrigation systems take water to fields, which help farmers grow crops all year round, not just in the rainy season.

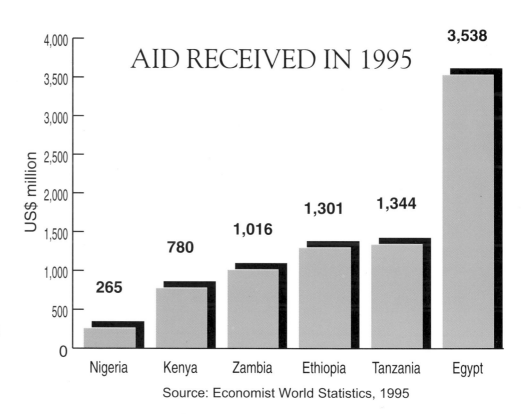

AID RECEIVED IN 1995

Source: Economist World Statistics, 1995

▲ Nigeria gets less help from abroad than other African countries.

HELP FOR WOMEN

In the early 1990s, a scheme was set up to help women in the countryside. The scheme spent money to help women learn to read and write. Once they could read, the women were able to find out about family planning, so that they did not have as many children. This meant there were less mouths to feed in each family and lives were easier.

Being able to read also helped women working in the fields, as they could read the instructions on seed packets and get better crops.

◀ Fulani women carry water, food and children across a river.

The dams and irrigation systems have helped some farmers, but not all. The dams cost so much money to build that farmers have to pay to use the irrigation. Only rich farmers can afford to pay for the irrigation. Many others have abandoned their farms to look for work in the cities.

◀ Only rich farmers can afford the sacks of fertilizers these lorries are carrying.

37

NEW FACTORIES

Much money has been spent building new, large factories so that Nigeria can produce goods itself, rather than buying them from other countries.

However, these factories use machinery instead of workers, so they do not provide employment for many people.

▼ This map shows where new factories have been built and the goods they produce.

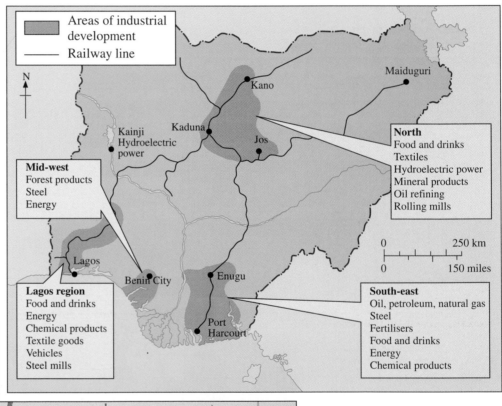

Areas of industrial development

Railway line

N

Kano

Maiduguri

Kaduna

Jos

Kainji Hydroelectric power

North
Food and drinks
Textiles
Hydroelectric power
Mineral products
Oil refining
Rolling mills

Mid-west
Forest products
Steel
Energy

0   250 km

0   150 miles

Lagos

Benin City

Enugu

Lagos region
Food and drinks
Energy
Chemical products
Textile goods
Vehicles
Steel mills

Port Harcourt

South-east
Oil, petroleum, natural gas
Steel
Fertilisers
Food and drinks
Energy
Chemical products

◀ This oil refinery was built so that Nigeria can process its own oil.

IMPROVING EDUCATION

In 1976, the government made education free for primary-school children and new schools were built in the cities and countryside.

SCHOOLS

'I want to pass my exams and go to work in an office in Lagos when I grow up.' Shehu, 8 years old.

In 1976, a national curriculum was set up so that all schools in Nigeria now teach the same subjects. Every child is taught two Nigerian languages as well as English.

In the north, Muslim children go to Islamic schools, where they are taught Arabic. They also learn to read the Qur'an, the Muslim holy book.

▲ Prayers at morning assembly in a primary school.

IMPROVING THE CITIES

In the 1970s, the government spent a lot of money on the cities, to try and improve the lives of people who lived there. New housing estates, hospitals and drains were built, and thousands of kilometres of new paved roads were laid, to link the cities together.

However, no money was spent on improving the railways, so all the traffic now depends on the roads. This causes problems in the rainy season, when the roads are often flooded.

▼ A new drain being built in Onitsha.

ABUJA: A NEW CAPITAL CITY

In 1976, building work started on a new capital city in central Nigeria called Abuja. A new capital was needed because Lagos was getting too crowded. Lagos had grown up from an old city, and the facilties had not been planned for so many people.

▶ A new conference centre in Abuja.

Abuja now has an international airport, luxury hotels, conference centres and industrial parks. Since 1976, more than 300,000 people have moved to Abuja, including the president in 1991.

Abuja is now the centre of government. More and more businesses and industries are moving there to use the city's facilities. The cost of living is high in Abuja, so only the rich can afford to live there.

THE FUTURE

Many people think that Nigeria needs a stable, democratic government to succeed in the future and to stop tribes fighting each other. Until then, people do not trust the government enough, which makes the government weaker.

▶ Major General Sani Abacha, who became Nigeria's president in 1993

42

◀ This simple irrigation scheme uses a hand tool called a shadoof. This technique can be used by many farmers because it is cheap.

SMALL-SCALE PROJECTS

Recently, several small-scale projects to help fight poverty have begun in Nigeria. These projects give advice to people such as farmers on how to change the way they work. The farmers can learn how to grow bigger crops, for example.

Smaller projects are cheaper than the large-scale projects of the 1970s, so they have been more successful because more people can afford them.

OIL PRODUCTION

Nigeria still has large oil and gas reserves to be used. There is enough oil to be pumped out for the next twenty-five years. The oil industry used to be completely controlled by the military government. Now that Nigerian companies are being allowed to enter the oil industry, as in other countries, they should make more money from it than the government by doing business with large foreign companies.

▲ A Nigerian oil rig.

RAIN FOREST PROTECTION

Over the last forty years, most of Nigeria's rain forest has been destroyed by its growing population and by forestry. The soil on the land has been washed away by the rains, making it no good for farming.

The government is now trying to protect the rain forest that is left. It is asking forestry teams to replant trees that they cut down. Trees and hedges are being planted around farmland, and manure is spread on to soil so that crops can grow.

Nigeria has many resources that can be used in the future, including its people. If they can be used with good planning, with a government the people want, Nigeria could become a much wealthier country in the future.

▲ Trees here were cut down for farm-land. The soil has now been washed away by the rains.

▶ Logging companies now have to replant the trees they cut down.

45

Glossary & Further information

GLOSSARY

Civil war Fighting between people in the same country.

Compound A group of houses in an enclosed space with shared facilities.

Delta An area at the mouth of some rivers where the river fans out into many smaller channels and deposits sand and mud.

Family planning The planning of the number of children to have.

Fertilizers Either natural or artificial substances added to soil to make it richer and better for growing crops.

Irrigation The artificial watering of the land to grow crops, using channels, sprinklers or pipes.

Literacy People's ability to read and write.

Plantations Large farms where a single crop is grown.

National Curriculum A list of subjects chosen by a country to be taught in all its schools.

Natural Resources Materials like oil, gas and foodcrops in a country.

Military Government A government where the army is in charge of all decisions concerning the country, and the people have little or no say in these decisions.

Raw Materials The first goods that a factory needs to make a product.

Silt A fertile, fine mud carried in rivers and deposited in a river valley during floods.

Tropical Rain Forest Areas of forest near the Equator where there is lots of rain.

BOOKS TO READ

Africa (Continents series) Wayland, 1997
Kenya (Country Insights series) Wayland, 1997
Trouble with Nigeria (African Writers series) Heinemann, 1984
Nigeria (Economically Developing Countries series) Wayland, 1996

RESOURCE MATERIALS

Ayida - Development and Change in Nigeria is a photopack with teachers' booklet. From Oxfam, 274 Banbury Road, Oxford OX2 7DZ.

ActionAid (Hamlyn House, Archway, London N19 5PG) is able to provide information on Nigeria.

The Development Education Association (3rd floor, Cowper Street, London EC2A 4AP) can provide further information on teaching packs.

Topic web and Development activities

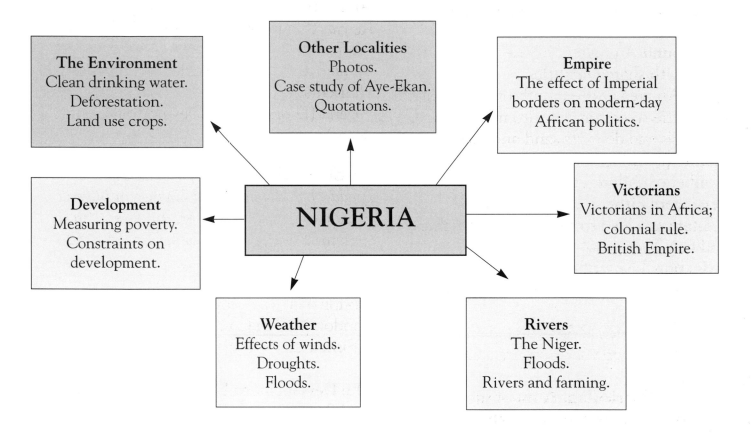

The Environment
Clean drinking water.
Deforestation.
Land use crops.

Other Localities
Photos.
Case study of Aye-Ekan.
Quotations.

Empire
The effect of Imperial borders on modern-day African politics.

Development
Measuring poverty.
Constraints on development.

NIGERIA

Victorians
Victorians in Africa; colonial rule.
British Empire.

Weather
Effects of winds.
Droughts.
Floods.

Rivers
The Niger.
Floods.
Rivers and farming.

FURTHER ACTIVITIES

<u>Measuring Poverty</u>
Use the photographs on pages 5, 19 and 35 to look at the kinds of construction that are used in Nigeria. What materials are used, and how do they compare with materials used in Britain? Now look at the National Mosque on page 21: how does it, and the buildings behind, compare with here? Can you draw any conclusions?

<u>Religion and Festivals</u>
Use the index to find the main religions in Nigeria. Find out the main festival days of those religions. (You could also get this information from the Nigerian High Commission, 9 Northumberland Ave, London WC2N 5BX.) Make up a festival diary on a map of Nigeria, so you can celebrate with the people of different regions on their festival days.

<u>Farming</u>
Use the table on page 23 as a starting place, and divide the class into the percentages given. Now get them to do a survey of what their parents do for a living. What percentage work in Agriculture?

Next time you go shopping in a supermarket, see if you can find any foods from Africa. Find the countries on a map in an atlas.

INDEX

Numbers in **bold** refer to pictures and text.